My World of Science

SHINY AND DULL

Angela Royston

Heinemann
LIBRARY

www.heinemann.co.uk/library
Visit our website to find out more information about **Heinemann Library** books.

To order:
☎ Phone 44 (0) 1865 888066
📄 Send a fax to 44 (0) 1865 314091
💻 Visit the Heinemann Bookshop at www.heinemann.co.uk/library to browse our catalogue and order online.

First published in Great Britain by Heinemann Library, Halley Court, Jordan Hill, Oxford OX2 8EJ, part of Harcourt Education.

Heinemann is a registered trademark of Harcourt Education Ltd.

Editorial: Andrew Farrow and Dan Nunn
Design: Jo Hinton-Malivoire and
    Tinstar Design Limited (www.tinstar.co.uk)
Picture Research: Maria Joannou and Sally Smith
Production: Viv Hichens

Originated by Blenheim Colour Ltd
Printed and bound in China by
    South China Printing Company

ISBN 0 431 13738 2
07 06 05 04 03
10 9 8 7 6 5 4 3 2 1

**British Library Cataloguing
in Publication Data**
Royston, Angela
Shiny and dull. – (My world of science)
1. Surfaces (Technology) – Optical properties –
Juvenile literature
I. Title
620.1'1295

A full catalogue record for this book is available from the British Library.

Acknowledgements
The publishers would like to thank the following for permission to reproduce photographs:
Corbis (RF) p. 22; Eye Ubiquitous pp. 23 (Anthea Beszant), 26 (Bennett Dean); Hulton Getty p. 19; Impact/Piers Cavendish p. 28; Photodisc pp. 4, 17; Powerstock/Zefa p. 29; Robert Harding p. 9; Science Photo Library pp. 14 (Robin Scagell), 27 (Tim Hazael); Shout p. 15; Trevor Clifford pp. 5, 6, 7, 8, 10, 11, 13, 16, 18, 21, 24, 25; Trip pp. 20 (Frank Blackburn), 12 (H. Rogers).

Cover photograph reproduced with permission of Trevor Clifford.

Every effort has been made to contact copyright holders of any material reproduced in this book. Any omissions will be rectified in subsequent printings if notice is given to the publishers.

Contents

Any words appearing in the text in bold, **like this**,
are explained in the Glossary.

Shiny or dull?

These bells are both shiny. You can
see that they are shiny because they
reflect the light.

These things are dull. Although the flowers have bright colours, they are still dull. They do not reflect as much light as the shiny bells.

Which is shinier?

The smoother something is, the shinier it is. The plastic **pepper grinder** is shiny. But the metal knob on top is smoother and shinier.

Some materials are shinier than other materials. These things are all quite shiny. But which is shinier — the wooden bowl or the silver paper? (Answer on page 31.)

Metals

Most things made of metal are smooth and shiny. But sometimes metals can be dull. Which of these metals is the dullest? (Answer on page 31.)

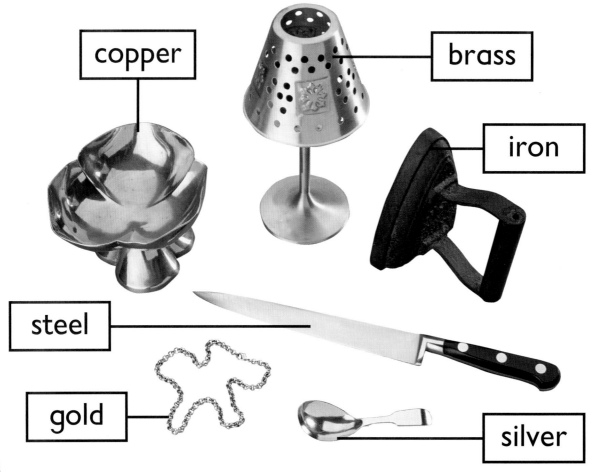

copper

brass

iron

steel

gold

silver

This toaster is very shiny. It is made of iron but it has been covered with a layer of **chrome**. Chrome makes the iron shiny.

Decorating with shiny things

Shiny things look more exciting than dull things. This is because shiny things **reflect** more light and attract attention. These children are decorating a wreath with shiny **tinsel** and coloured balls.

Clothes are often made to look more beautiful by adding shiny things. This girl's scarf is decorated with **sequins**. The boy's T-shirt has a shiny shape on the front.

Reflecting light

Shiny things **gleam** because light **reflects** off them. This means that light bounces straight off them. When the Sun's rays hit them, they gleam like the Sun.

Dull things are slightly rough, just like the saddle of this bicycle. Light bounces off it in many different directions. This makes it look dull.

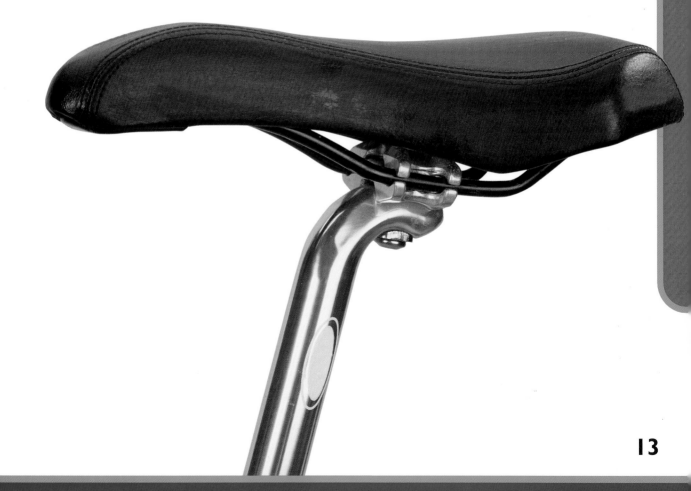

Reflecting light at night

Shiny things can be useful at night. These shiny **cats' eyes** reflect the **headlights** of each car. They show the middle of the road ahead.

This man's jacket has shiny strips attached to it. The strips reflect the lights of cars and lorries. This helps drivers to see the man in the dark.

Mirrors

Some things are so shiny you can see yourself in them. You can see yourself in a mirror. The mirror **reflects** all the light straight back at you.

Water and very shiny metals can sometimes act like a mirror. The water in this lake is so smooth it reflects the people and the boat.

Dull materials

These things are all dull. They are dull because they are slightly rough. They may feel smooth, but there are tiny bumps on their surface.

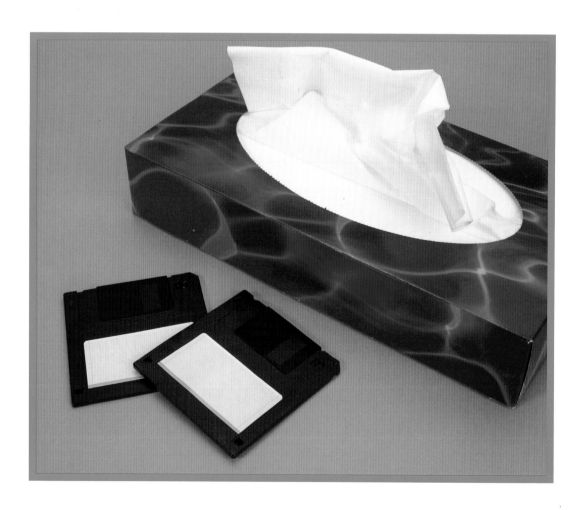

Many things are naturally dull. This house is built of bricks, which are dull. The roof has dull tiles on it. The trees are all dull too.

Which is duller?

The mouse is more dull than the wheat. Some birds and other animals would like to eat the mouse. Being dull helps the mouse to hide from them.

The bag is duller than the lunch box. The jumper is the dullest thing in this photo. Which is duller – the spoon or the carton? (Answer on page 31.)

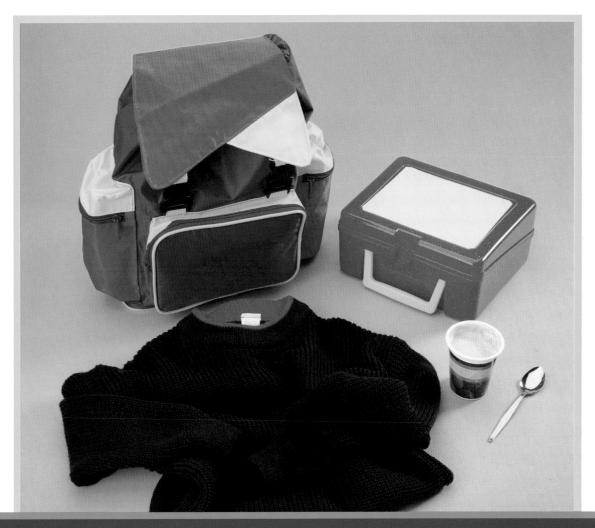

Dull can be useful

Roads are covered with dull, rough **tar**. The dullness stops light reflecting from the road into the drivers' eyes. The roughness stops the cars from slipping.

Dull things do not stand out as much as shiny things. The dustbin is dull because it is not very beautiful to look at.

How shiny things become dull

If some metal things are not cleaned, they become dull. The dirt stops them from shining. Iron things sometimes become **rusty**. This makes them become even duller.

These shoes have become dirty and dull. Shoes have to be cleaned with special shoe cleaner. Leather shoes become shinier if you rub them with a cloth.

Making dull things shiny

This man is painting the iron railings. The paint will make them smooth and shiny. It will also keep out the rain. This will stop the railings from going **rusty**.

This wood is being covered with a layer of **varnish**. The varnish will make the wood shinier. It will also protect it from water.

Polishing

This car was dirty and dull. Rubbing it with special **polish** removes the dirt and makes it clean and shiny again.

Stones are usually very dull. Some are polished to make them smooth and shiny. These stones have been polished until they shine brightly.

Glossary

cats' eyes small pieces of glass set in the road. The glass reflects light so car drivers can see the middle of the road.

chrome a kind of shiny metal that is used to cover iron and steel

gleam to shine

headlights the lights on the front of cars, trucks and other vehicles. Headlights light up the road in front of vehicles at night. They warn other vehicles that they are there.

pepper grinder a small machine for grinding peppercorns into powder

polish stuff that makes some things smooth and shiny

reflect bounce off in one direction

rusty covered in a flaky, reddish-brown coating

sequins flat, shiny disc or spangle that is sewn onto clothes

tar black stuff used to make the top layer of many roads

tinsel short threads of shiny metal that are joined in a string

varnish liquid like a clear paint

Answers

page 7
The silver paper is shinier than the wooden bowl.

page 8
Iron is the dullest metal.

page 21
The carton is duller than the spoon.

Index

Titles in the *My World of Science* series include:

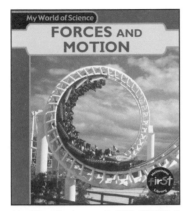

Hardback   0 431 13700 5

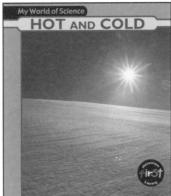

Hardback   0 431 13715 3

Hardback   0 431 13712 9

Hardback   0 431 13704 8

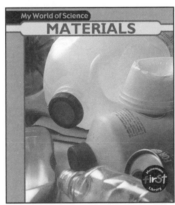

Hardback   0 431 13701 3

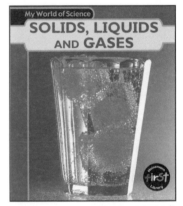

Hardback   0 431 13702 1

Hardback   0 431 13714 5

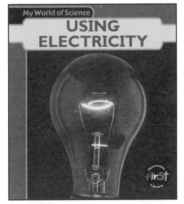

Hardback   0 431 13716 1

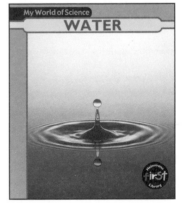

Hardback   0 431 13703 X

Find out about the other titles in this series on our website www.heinemann.co.uk/library